Published by Creative Education
123 South Broad Street, Mankato, Minnesota 56001
Creative Education is an imprint of The Creative Company

Designed by Stephanie Blumenthal

Photographs by Joan Balzarini, Robert Barber,
Craig Davis, Carrol Henderson, Tom Stack & Associates
(Erwin & Peggy Bauer, Bill Everitt, Joe McDonald, Peter Mead,
Brian Parker, John Shaw, Therisa Stack, Dave Watts)

Library of Congress Cataloging-in-Publication Data

Rabinowitz, Sima.
Parrots / by Sima Rabinowitz
p. cm. — (Let's investigate)
ISBN 1-58341-196-8
1. Parrots—Juvenile literature. [1. Parrots.]
I. Title. II. Let's investigate (Mankato, Minn.)
QL696.P7 R32   2001
598.7'1—dc21   00-064474

First edition

2 4 6 8 9 .7 5 3 1

PARROTS

SIMA RABINOWITZ

Creative ☀ Education

PARROT
HISTORY

Parrots are ancient birds. Scientific evidence shows that they existed as far back as 40 million years ago.

When we think of parrots, most of us think of talking birds, and it's true that some parrots can mimic human speech. But it's important to remember that even when kept as pets, parrots are still wild birds, not domestic animals like dogs or cats. Every parrot species that is sold as a pet developed in the wild.

Right, an Australian king parrot
Far right, two rainbow lories

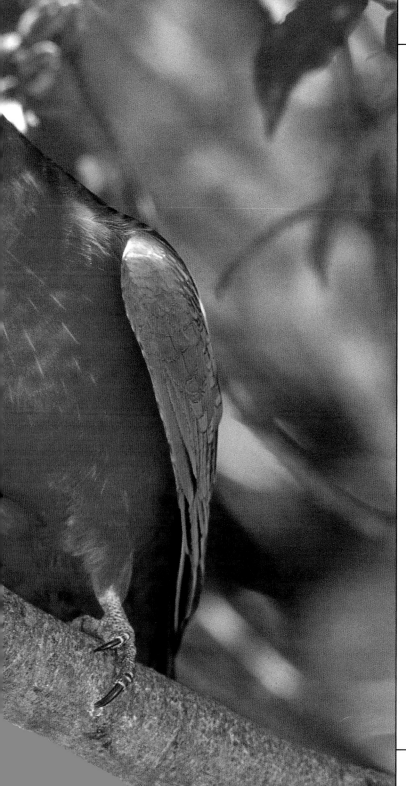

P arrots have lived in the wild for millions of years. With their beautiful colors and unusual voices, they are some of nature's most magnificent wild birds.

PARROT
HEART

Bird hearts beat much faster than human hearts. A human heart beats approximately 72 times per minute. A bird heart beats approximately 220 times per minute.

PARROT

RELATIVES

Although there are more than 350 species of parrots around the world, with different colors, sizes, and habits, all parrots resemble each other. They are not, however, considered to be the relatives of any other group of birds.

Above, the galah cockatoo of Australia Right, a rain forest, home to a variety of parrots

PARROTS AS BIRDS

Parrots are **native** to every continent in the world except Europe. More than 350 different species, or types, of parrots (*Psittaciformes*) have adapted to a wide range of wild places, from the jungles and woodlands of Africa to the humid rain forests of South America.

All parrots have large heads, stubby necks, and short legs. No matter what their size or color, parrots are easy to distinguish from other birds because of these characteristics.

PARROT
P Y G M Y

The smallest parrots in the world are pygmy parrots of New Guinea. Some of them are only four inches (10 cm) long.

Above, the endangered orange-bellied parrot Left, a military macaw

PARROT

Parrots in different regions of the same forest develop their own dialects, or speech patterns. **Ornithologists** *can determine where a captured bird came from by listening to its dialect.*

8

Around the world, parrots of all types are famous for their extraordinary voices. Many parrots squawk, shriek, or scream. The short-tailed parrot in the rain forests along the Amazon River in South America makes a noise like a horn while it feeds. The mulga parrot in Australia makes an unusual *chweet-chweet-chweet* sound when it's flying. Several types of hanging parrots are known for their high-pitched voices.

Right, two blue and gold macaws
Far right, the north island kaka of New Zealand

A parrot's calls are a way of communicating with other members of its flock. A parrot can tell other parrots where food is located, or it can warn them that enemies are nearby.

Like all birds, parrots have certain characteristics that set them apart from other animal groups. Feathers are the most important of these. A bird's feathers weigh two to three times as much as its bones.

PARROT
SPEECH

Alex, an African gray parrot raised at the University of Arizona, learned to recognize and name 100 objects, to count to six, and to say dozens of phrases. If Alex bit someone, he would sometimes say, "I'm sorry."

PARROT

Birds use about 50 muscles to fly. In general, the bigger a bird's wings, the slower the wings beat to keep the bird in flight. Parrots and other birds use their tails to steer, but each wing can also act independently to help the bird change direction.

CLIMBING & EATING

The large feathers at the tips of a bird's wings, called primaries, make it possible for birds to fly. The primaries act like the propellers on a plane. Because of their angle at the wings' tips, the primaries push against the pressure of the wind and help the bird to lift itself into the air. Birds use their wings and tail to steer as they fly. Most parrots can fly, but unlike many other kinds of birds, parrots are also exceptional climbers.

A flock of red and green macaws taking flight

Parrots need to keep their hooked bills sharp for climbing and grabbing food. They sharpen their bills by gnawing on wood. This gnashing makes a small cracking noise.

11

P arrots have a hooked bill, which is also called a beak. These powerful hooked bills help parrots climb through the branches of trees. A parrot uses the strong curve of its bill to latch onto a branch, then it pulls itself upward, climbing from branch to branch. In this way, the parrot's bill is almost like a third foot.

Above, a macaw sharpening its bill Left, the head of a grand electus parrot

PARROT
YAWN

Parrots yawn often, and their yawns, like human yawns, are infectious—when one parrot starts to yawn, others will, too.

A red-winged parrot having lunch

A parrot also uses its bill to grab and shell the seeds and nuts it eats. The parrot grasps the food with its bill, crushes the outer shell, and swallows the seed inside. Then, it lets the shell fall to the ground.

A parrot's beak is an effective food crusher. It is made of a very hard substance called keratin, the same substance that forms human fingernails.

The unique design of the parrot's jaw contributes to the beak's effectiveness. The lower mandible, or jaw, moves, but the upper mandible does not. This lets the parrot hold small nuts and seeds steady as it crushes them.

PARROT
D I E T

Some of the seeds that parrots eat can be poisonous to them. To counteract the effects of the poison, parrots eat riverbank clay that is rich in neutralizing chemicals.

Above, a macaw plucking seeds Left, a parrot feeds itself using its feet and beak

Parrots cannot chew, so they have to swallow their food whole. Once it has been swallowed, the food passes into an organ called the crop. The crop is like an elastic pouch. It produces a liquid called crop milk, which moistens the food and makes it tender. Once the food is soft, it passes from the crop into the gizzard.

The gizzard does for birds what jaws and teeth do for mammals. It crushes and grinds the food so it can be digested in the **intestines**.

PARROT
RARITY

In the Andes Mountains of Ecuador and Colombia, the yellow-eared parrot nests in the trunk of the wax palm tree. Wax palms are the tallest trees in the world. Unfortunately, so many of them have been cut down that only about 50 remain.

15

Seeds, berries, and nuts are king parrot favorites

PARROT

SILENCE

*Even though parrots are very noisy birds, they can be exceptionally quiet when they eat. Parrots eat so slowly and quietly that their movements often go unnoticed. This is a way of protecting themselves from **predators**.*

Right, a citron cockatoo eating a nut
Far right, a parakeet with an itch

A parrot's feet also play an important role in the way the parrot eats. Parrots are zygodactyls, birds with some toes that point forward and some toes that point backward. The first and fourth toes on a parrot's foot point backward. The second and third toes point forward.

The parrot relies on its toes when it climbs, perches, eats, and even sleeps. Thanks to its toes, a parrot can balance on one foot while it grabs a shell or nut with the other foot. Then, still standing on one leg, it can lift the foot that holds the food up to its beak.

Eating is not the only thing parrots do on one leg. They also sleep on one leg, tucking the other under their belly.

Some scientists believe that parrots have tiny cells on their ankles, knees, and leg joints that sense vibrations. These cells may help them recognize when a predator is near.

19

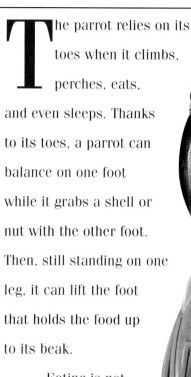

Above, a jaguar, a parrot's natural enemy
Left, special toes enable parrots to balance on one foot
Far left, a sleeping parakeet

PARROT
NESTS

The monk parakeet, also known as the Quaker parrot, is native to Bolivia, Colombia, Argentina, and Paraguay. Rather than nest in the holes of trees, monk parakeets nest on the branches.

A camouflaged yellow-naped parrot in Costa Rica

LIFE IN THE TREES

Most wild parrots live in trees. They **nest** in the holes of tree trunks and feed on the wide variety of plants that grow in wooded areas. However, not all parrots live in the same kind of trees or in the same type of **habitat**.

Many parrots live in the rain forests along the Amazon River in Brazil and Paraguay, in South America. Here, parrots use their excellent climbing skills to make their way through the thick **foliage**.

The most common color for parrots in the rain forest is green. This is protective coloring. If a parrot senses that it is in danger, it can fly into the trees for camouflage.

Parrots of many other colors can also be found in the rain forests of South America. One of the largest is the hyacinth macaw. This bright blue bird is one of the biggest parrots in the world. It is almost 40 inches (1 m) long. Large birds have a longer lifespan than small birds, and hyacinth macaws often live for more than 100 years.

PARROT
FEATHERS

Parrots molt once a year. Their feathers fall off and new ones grow. This is a slow process. Only one or two feathers molt at a time so the bird's ability to fly won't be impaired. It can take up to two months for a large parrot to molt completely.

Above, feather detail of a red macaw

PARROT

*Wild parrots current-
ly live in Hyde Park,
a suburb of Chicago,
Illinois. These par-
rots make their nests
on branches, electri-
cal poles, and even
satellite dishes!*

Not all parrots live in the rain forest, though. In Australia, some species of parrots live in lightly wooded areas along the edges of farm-land. Others live in parks, gardens, and along the sides of roads.

One of the most common parrots in Australia is the cockatiel. This beautiful bird has an extremely long tail, which accounts for one-third of the entire length of its body.

The woods of Australia and the rain forests of South America are home to many kinds of parrots. A wide variety of parrots is also found in the mountains of India and China, in the dry woodlands of southern Africa, and in the forests of Mexico.

PARROT
STRENGTH

The strongest parrot in the world is the aggressive kea, which lives in New Zealand. It has been known to do all kinds of strange things, including tearing the windshield wipers off of cars.

*Left, two cockatiels
Far left, the Australian
ringneck parrot*

PARROT

Pet parrots in California have been known to become agitated before an earthquake—probably because they are more sensitive to tremor vibrations than humans are.

25

PARROT FLOCKS

Parrots live in flocks, or groups. Members of a flock will nest, feed, bathe, **roost**, and sleep near each other. Within their flocks, parrots live in pairs and mate for life with one partner.

One important activity that helps keep a flock together is called preening. Preening is a process of cleaning and straightening a bird's feathers. Parrots spend a lot of time preening themselves, but they also preen each other. Sometimes they do this to develop strong bonds, but sometimes they preen each other for comfort when they are in stressful situations.

Left, a flock of crimson rosella and king parrots Far left, a conure, a parrot native to the Americas, preening

PARROT

GIFT

26

MATING AND REPRODUCING

Because parrots mate for life, their courtship rituals are very important. Courtship rituals are behaviors that help a pair get to know each other and develop a close relationship. A pair of courting parrots will spend a lot of time preening each other, and the male bird will feed the female. This is a way for him to practice the important task of feeding their babies.

A male parrot feeding his mate

P arrots mature, or become adults, between their second and fourth years. When a parrot matures, it is ready to mate and **breed**. Parrots breed once a year.

Like all birds, parrots lay eggs. But most parrots don't have to work at preparing the nest for their babies. The female parrot simply lays her eggs in a tree hole.

PARROT
E G G S

Egg color varies from species to species, but all birds that nest in holes—including parrots—lay white eggs.

27

*Above, three-week-old conures
Left, a Major Mitchell's cockatoo in a tree hole*

PARROT

Chicks hatch by using the only tooth they'll ever have, the egg tooth, to puncture the shell. The egg tooth is a sharp, pointed tooth on the upper beak. After the chick emerges from its shell, the egg tooth falls off.

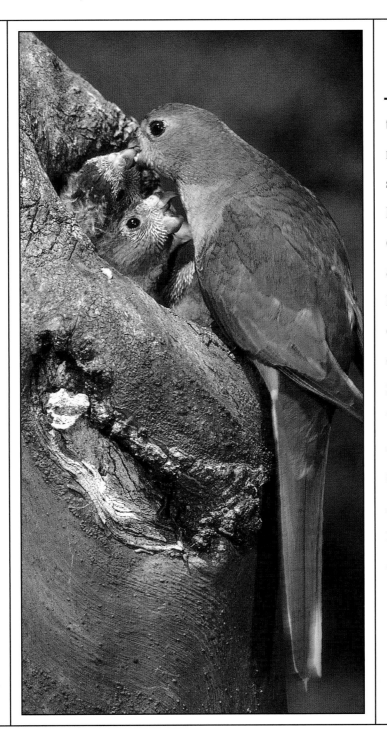

A male orange-bellied parrot feeding his chicks

A female parrot lays only two or three eggs, then she broods in the nest. This means that she sits on the eggs to keep them warm so the chicks inside will grow and develop properly. Depending on what type of parrot laid them, the eggs will **hatch** in 21 to 30 days. While she broods, the female parrot does not leave the nest. She stays perfectly still and her mate feeds her. He will also feed the chicks once they hatch.

Chicks are born with their eyes closed and without feathers. They can't fly or sit up by themselves and are completely dependent on their parents for food and protection.

In some species, chicks are ready to leave the nest after only one month. Other kinds of parrot chicks may remain in the nest for as long as three months. During this time, their feathers grow and the birds get strong enough to fly and to eat on their own. In a few years, they will mature, find mates, and breed.

PARROT
EYES

Parrots have excellent sight and can spot things on the ground from great heights. Their eyes can move independently of each other. This is called monocular vision.

29

*Above, the Mexican red-fronted parrot
Left, a blue and gold macaw*

PARROT
RARITY

The rarest parrot in the world is the spix macaw in northeastern Brazil. There is only one known spix macaw left in the wild today.

Right, the crimson rosella of eastern Australia
Far right, lorikeets and other parrots are endangered around the world

ENDANGERED PARROTS

The parrot family has more **endangered** species than any other family of birds. At least 90 species of parrots are threatened. One threat they face is destruction of their habitat. Extensive logging and agricultural land clearing are quickly destroying forests and woods around the world.

Another serious problem is that too many parrots are captured from their native habitats to be sold as pets. Parrots are beautiful and fascinating birds. Many species can be tamed and can become very affectionate. Unfortunately, parrots have become so popular as pets that they may become **extinct** in the wild.

Conservationists around the world are working together to protect parrots and their habitats, for once the woods where parrots live are destroyed, these amazing wild birds will be lost, too.

Glossary

To **breed** is to have babies.

Species that are **endangered** are at risk of becoming extinct.

A species that is **extinct** no longer has any living members on the planet.

A mass of leaves is called **foliage**.

A **habitat** is the place where an animal or plant naturally lives and grows.

Baby birds **hatch** when they break out of their shells.

The **intestines** are part of an animal's digestive tract.

Animals and people who are **native** to a particular place or habitat have always lived there.

A female bird will **nest** by staying in the hole where she makes her home and sitting on top of her eggs.

Ornithologists are people who study birds.

A **predator** is an animal that kills and eats other animals.

To **roost** is to rest on a perch or in a nest.

Index